A. JODOROWSKY · KAZAN

The way Jodorowsky explained Tarot to his Cat

LO SCARABEO

The way Jodorowsky explained Tarot to his Cat

A book by Alejandro Jodorowsky
with the collaboration of Kazan, the cat
Illustrations by Christian Gaudin
Foreword by Daniele Palmieri

Graphic and layout: Chiara Demagistris
Editing: Elena Delmastro, Riccardo Minetti,
Lunaea Weatherstone

Original Title: Le Tarot des Chats
© 2012 - Alejandro Jodorowsky
© 2021 - Lo Scarabeo

The cards of the Marseille Tarot are from:
Marseille Tarot - Professional Edition
by Anna Maria Morsucci and Mattia Ottolini

www.loscarabeo.com
info@loscarabeo.com
Facebook & Instagram: LoScarabeoTarot

Printed by TGS in 2021
All rights reserved.

TABLE of CONTENTS

Foreword - *The Feline Art of Divination with the Cards*	5
The Fool	9
The Magician	11
The High Priestess	13
The Empress	15
The Emperor	17
The Hierophant	19
The Lover	21
The Chariot	23
Justice	25
The Hermit	27
The Wheel of Fortune	29
Strength	31
The Hanged Man	33
XIII	37
Temperance	41
The Devil	45
The Tower	49
The Star	53
The Moon	57
The Sun	61
Judgement	65
The World	69
Appendix - *Tarot of Cats and Tarot of Marseille*	73
Biography - *Alejandro Jodorowsky*	77
Foreword Author - *Daniele Palmieri*	79

FOREWORD

The Feline Art of Divination with the Cards

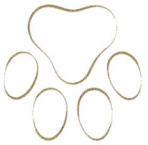

"How blind can one be?" Kazan must have thought when he caused the Tarot de Marseilles to fall from the library shelf exactly when Jodorowsky was trying to penetrate the hidden secrets of the Minor Arcana. "A coincidence I would dare to define as miraculous," Jodorowsky wrote in *The Way of the Tarot*, remembering how as he knelt to pick up and sort out the cards strewn on the ground, he found himself looking at the Ace of Cups. And the hidden meaning of the entire deck was revealed to him.

Knowing the feline soul, we can agree this was not a simple synchronicity. If we could flip the perspective and see through Kazan's eyes, we would understand how the cat deliberately decided to awaken the creative intuition of his human to reveal the secrets of the ancient art of divination. Cats have protected these mysteries since the time of ancient Egypt, where felines were venerated alongside the goddess Bastet, the high priestess of the hidden side of all things.

It is perhaps this obscure tradition to which Court de Gébelin referred when he traced the twenty-two Major Arcana of the Tarot de Marseilles to the wisdom of Egypt—once again a lost wisdom, as no Tarot expert or philologist believes his theories anymore. Precisely for this reason, perhaps, Kazan's work with Jodorowsky is not yet finished. It continues day by day, from that first impact between the Tarot cards and the floor up until the creation of this deck, where he is the protagonist, both in the images and in the text. Having given his human a free hand at first, Kazan, dissatisfied with the results, decided to apply the subtle practice of thought manipulation that cats use to condition the behavior of humans. It is not difficult to imagine him crouching at night next to his sleeping human, whispering insights about the cards into his unsuspecting ears.

"My dear Kazan, after all these years I have decided to thank you by explaining the Tarot to you too." Jodorowsky must have said this on wakening after the first night of feline whispers, not realizing that each word he then said and wrote was narrated the night before by the cat. Through Kazan's wise words and revelations, the feline art of divination with the cards could once again be revived among the people.

"For my faithful companion of seventeen years, Kazan, the cat who has forgotten he is a cat and believes he is my son."

— *Alejandro Jodorowsky*

THE FOOL

I have no master. I go where I want, eat when I want, sleep when I want. The street belongs to me. The trees are mine. The rubbish heaps, the ruins, the sky, the sun, the moon, the stars—all belong to me. And above all, the mice are mine.

When I need to sacrifice one to fill my empty stomach, I do it with respect, like a game. I pursue it until the understanding, tired rodent says to me:

"It will be a pleasure for me to be eaten by you, because I will enter into your body and be transformed into you. I will never again be afraid." It's true, I am afraid of nothing. When I change into a ball of spiky hair, arch my back, and hiss threateningly, even dogs run away.

I admit I dislike order, and I am not a domestic cat but an independent cat. I love the outdoor life so much—rolling on the rooftops and eating my fleas, I purr nonstop. But beware: I can bite, scratch, and with one swipe of my claws, tear out the eyes of anyone who tries to take away my freedom.

If you have drawn this card, it could mean:
A great journey, imagination, joie de vivre, liberation, a burst of energy, vagabondage, authenticity.

THE MAGICIAN

I am young. Full of immense energy, I take my first steps in the world. Everything that moves gains my attention. In this apartment, far removed from nature, where no real tree grows and the presence of a mouse would be a miracle, my masters amuse themselves by throwing me a stuffed toy rodent or a rubber snake. They watch and admire me. Because I love having an audience. I pretend to be fooled and jump on the toy, showing off my agility. Thanks to this, they love me. They give me delicious pieces of chicken and let me sleep with them.

I have all the qualities of a healthy cat: speed, iron muscles, flexibility, and above all, a good attention span. When something interests me, I focus on it with such intensity that it alone exists in the center of a fading world. I know this attention is essential, because my life depends on my choices. The future is uncertain, it could be good or bad, and I have in my claws the capacity to create the path that suits me the most: to be a fat domestic slave or run away and become a bandit or find work as a magician's assistant. But these are all plans for the future. For now, I am diving into the present and only care about developing my capabilities.

If you have drawn this card, it could mean:

A beginning, a player, astuteness, multiple talents, the ability to choose, new undertakings, hesitation.

THE HIGH PRIESTESS

In my eyes the most important thing is dignity. When I have licked every part of my body to make my coat as clean and shining as the light of the moon, nestled in my preferred chair, I resemble a stone statue. In ancient Egypt, the pharaohs worshiped my ancestors as gods. I consider myself sacred. I can see in the dark every detail of everything around me. Nothing seems mysterious.

When the television is on, I can watch for hours these worlds going by that are so similar to my dreams. I have no need to hunt. What's the point? Chasing after a common field mouse is undignified. My servant believes herself to be my lover: she offers me appetizing dishes. I accept, pretending a great disdain. While she watches me, I pick at small pieces. Once she leaves me in peace, I devour my food with great speed. Do you wish me to give you some magical power? Kneel before me and recognize that I am the ruler of this house that you believe is yours.

If you have drawn this card, it could mean:

A religious spirit, a magical woman, isolation, a severe mother, tradition, purity, secrecy.

THE EMPRESS

I am beautiful. Everyone wants to caress me. When I arch my back and mew like a young girl, serious faces light up with a smile of satisfaction. It is impossible not to love me. My masters feel my vital life force, but they have no idea of the magnitude of my fertility. If I decided to become a mother, I could give birth ceaselessly and populate the world with kittens. I am the queen of seductresses.

On nights of the full moon, I am transformed by its light into a phosphorescent goddess. I go out on the balcony and begin a deep caterwauling of a love song. Males tremble, feeling winter transforms into a hot spring. They fight each other and with throaty warbling throw me their promises: "Jump down to the street, run away with me, I will be your slave, I will hunt for you, I offer you the world!"

I admit these voices tempt me, but I am wary. The enthusiasm of these romantic beasts may be fleeting. Although I am filled with immense fervor—ready to vanquish any limits, to feed at my breast a river of beautiful felines, to cover the entire planet with their silken bodies, and so become the ruler of the world—I control myself. I hide my fire under an apparent coldness. It is enough that my masters only find me beautiful, ignoring the miraculous extent of my creative power. One day, a king will come, overcoming my coldness, who will know how to seduce me. I am certain that he will come.

If you have drawn this card, it could mean:
Fertility, seduction, artistic creativity, coquetry, beauty, abundance, growth.

THE EMPEROR

I am a strong and well-balanced gentleman. I have a thick coat, a hard head supported by a bullish neck, and four paws that land on the ground with the greatest confidence. No rival can bring me down. In vain they throw themselves against me, while I remain stable and immovable. If I wanted to, I could kill them with one bite, but why waste my energy on inferior animals when my authority is already established throughout the neighborhood? I don't need to make any effort to be obeyed. My masters can leave the doors open and delicious dishes on the kitchen table, and no feline thief would dare enter. When I go for a stroll in the park, everyone moves out of my path. They leave me the best tree branches and lay before my claws a tasty mouse or a tender little bird, and then back away, purring and curtseying. Before entering my home, I carefully lick my rich fur and then, all clean, I return with dignity to the velvet-covered chair that was given to me as my royal bed.

All the cats in the neighborhood beg me to be the father of their children. My authority and my ability to protect them are seductive. My masters' little daughters feel safe from bad dreams when I sleep in their beds. They know my powerful gaze can dissolve any nightmare monster.

If you have drawn this card, it could mean:
The capacity to protect, stability, economic security, authority, a powerful father, the application of the law, tyranny.

THE HIEROPHANT

I am extraordinarily lucky. My owners adore me. This is natural: I can see what they are not capable of seeing. The house is full of invisible phantoms that want to communicate with humans but cannot. They talk to me and send me their messages of love. I pass them on to my masters by means of soft growls, staring at a fixed point in space. My masters understand that place holds the spirit of one who has passed. As it is impossible to caress a ghost who has no flesh, they caress me. Through me the phantoms receive the affection and rejoice in it. I feel imbued with a magical mission. My slightest movement has a sacred dignity. I bless everything I hear, everything I see, everything I smell.

When my master leaves me alone in the house, I allow all the hungry cats in the neighborhood to eat the leftover food in the kitchen bin. I also share with them the biscuits and pâté that are generously offered to me every day. The poor things eat until they are full, licking their whiskers, repeating a meow that sounds almost human: "Papa, Papa…" They see me as a father to them. And they are right because I see each of them as my favorite child. I must confess, however, to my overwhelming desire to dominate, bite, steal, and murder mice. But I overcome these impulses and conceal my dark side—and pass for a being inhabited only by light.

If you have drawn this card, it could mean:
An ideal union, a false or sincere master, religious dogma, self-control, a blessing, expansive vision.

THE LOVER

I think I was born laughing. I have always been overcome by the joy of living. Everything makes me happy: nature with its colors and perfumes, the odorless earth where I do my daily business, the little birds that make my mouth water, the flies I push against the windowpane, frightening them just to enjoy their buzzing—in short, life in all its infinite forms. Lines from my heart connect me to all creation.

Ah, meow, meow, the pleasure of loving!

Every sensation, friendly or aggressive, produces ecstasy in me. Fighting can build relationships. With more than one neighbor, we scratched and scuffled and then became the best friends in the world.

I am very cunning: when two beautiful females throw me bewitching glances and invite me to choose one or the other, why should I sacrifice my romantic inclinations? I see both of them at different times, promising them my exclusive caresses. It is one thing to promise, and another to do what you love! My heart is huge, I can love the whole world. I am a kind of archer who shoots his arrows at everything his senses can perceive. When I have an admirer who is madly in love with me, I get into her mind like a hurricane of heat. I push from her meowing any criticism, aggression, comparison, contempt—all the shades of pride preventing total union, which then fills her body with the penetrating vibration of love.

If you have drawn this card, it could mean:
Joy, social life, doing what you love to do, pleasure, friendship, emotional conflict, choice.

THE CHARIOT

Advance, advance, advance: this is my only desire. To go as far as possible, to conquer the world. I have no fear of leaving my home and being on the road. When their vacation arrives, my owners leave on a trip. I meow plaintively until they decide to take me with them. I settle in the car and enjoy watching the trees, houses, and poles that seem to gallop toward the past. Me, I happily head toward the future. I match my purrs to the purrs of the engine and imagine that mile by mile I am taking possession of the fields, the hills, the clouds, the people, and the entire earth. I was born to be king of the world, and even if this is only a dream, in my soul it is a reality. Oh, how I admire myself! How I love me! I am glad to be me and not one of those poor cats who live their whole lives closed up indoors! The young cats, seduced by my self-confidence, approach my noble body and rub against me, gently meowing until I lick their fur. This admiration feeds my dreams and gives me the invincible strength of a great ideal.

If you have drawn this card, it could mean:

Victory, a journey, worldly activities, confidence, intensity, seduction, war.

JUSTICE

I feel perfect. Nothing needs to be taken from me, nothing needs to be added. I am what I am, not what others would like me to be. No one forces me to eat what I don't want to eat—if they don't offer me morsels of fresh tuna, I declare a hunger strike. I demand my litter tray to have perfumed sand—if they put normal dirt, I protest by depositing my feces on an armchair or in the middle of the kitchen. And don't ask me to entertain an unpleasant visitor! If he dares to touch me, I bristle and hiss as furiously as if facing a hungry wolf. On the other hand, if someone merits my consideration, there are no limits to the expression of my feelings. I rub against his legs, purr ceaselessly, put my front paws on his knees. When he takes me in his arms, I snuggle against his chest, lick his hands, and give his fingers tiny bites, offering my belly to be caressed. I repay kindness but punish errors. I am an exemplary mother, full of milk and kindness, but I can also be severe. If one of my little ones urinates where they should not, I take them in my powerful jaws by the scruff,shake them, and rub their nose into the wet smell. Most important is to do myself justice and give myself what I deserve.

If you have drawn this card, it could mean:
Perfection, discipline, a severe mother, to receive what you deserve, a critical mind, a pregnant woman.

THE HERMIT

I have learned a lot from life. I have scars, memories of claws and bites, furless patches left by scabs, a stiff leg from a fall from a terrace while I was trying to catch a pigeon. I have my master's name and address tattooed inside my left ear. Age has made me cautious. I never walk in the open but move like a shadow, keeping close to walls. I do not allow myself to be surprised anymore by guard dogs or alley cats. They always need to demonstrate that they are the bosses of their own miserable hiding places. I don't tire myself chasing after a meal. I know how to remain as still as a dry branch on a tree, holding my breath as long as necessary. My heart beats soundlessly, my mouth is open, without drool. And look, a small bird or a mouse comes near me. There is always a curious one who comes to offer itself to my teeth. I snap my jaws faster than anyone can see. I chew discreetly, and when I have swallowed the delicious croquette, I once again open my mouth. Ability works better than force.

If you have drawn this card, it could mean:

Prudence, wisdom, humility, a secret master, solitude, detachment, saving energy.

THE WHEEL OF FORTUNE

I am staying with a kind veterinarian. This nice man has advertised me thus: "Beautiful angora cat. Free." I wait tranquilly for my new master. I won't entertain thoughts of failure—for me, this is just a change of patron. I have already had three. The first was an elderly lady in whose home I was born, who soon decided to go to heaven. The second was a young couple who treated me very well for a year, but the day they decided to go on vacation they abandoned me in a park. The third, the park warden, found me and gave me to his daughter. She was a nasty child. She pulled my tail, my whiskers, climbed with me to the top of the stairs and threw me down to see me land on all fours. I had to run away. Luckily, this veterinarian took me in. I have faith in the future. This world, which seems solid, is constantly changing. Things can get better or worse. What begins ends, and what ends begins. My next masters will be good, I know. They will love me and give me food in abundance. I will begin the best part of my life.

If you have drawn this card, it could mean:

The end of a cycle, a new beginning, the need for help, a blockage, reincarnation, financial gain, change.

STRENGTH

It is difficult for someone who has never lived this experience to imagine it in all its intensity. I am used to relaxing in front of the fire, imagining that the sparks thrown from the flaming wood are appetizing fireflies. When I devour one of these insects, I take in its body, but I also feel I am swallowing its light. (As you can see, I am very spiritual.) My body is elegant, my tail long and thin, my claws delicate and almost transparent. A true fairy. But when the lightning bolt of instinct strikes, I am transformed. My paws push against the earth with an incredible force, my back arches, traversed by waves like a furious ocean, and from the depth of my throat emerges a deafening howl, raucous and hot. Driven by this desire, I perceive, with an infallible intuition, where I can find what I need. Even if I am forbidden to go outside, I jump to the first open window and land in the treetops. From there I throw myself toward another building and, with phenomenal energy, climb up the wall, where I am awaited impatiently by the father of my future children. In this moment of grace when my spiritual nature gives way to my animal nature, I fear nothing. I allow myself to see, hear, feel, caress, and taste everything I desire.

If you have drawn this card, it could mean:

Creative instinct, new energy, strength, courage, the relationship between the mind and instinct, the call of sexuality, a battle with oneself.

THE HANGED MAN

Do not talk to me about the world. Nor about rodents, beautiful cats, or tree trunks so tall as to reach the sky if you climb them. Great tasty flies, leave me alone, do not distract me! Curled upside down, immobile, I do not pass my rough tongue over any part of my coat. I disdain the food that is placed near my nose. My masters, who love me as if I were their own child, are afraid that I am sick. I am not! Even if no one believes this, I am meditating. I am tired of being a vain and satisfied fat cat, sure of getting anything I want just by purring. I am a ferocious animal that has remained in a fetal state. I have not yet been born. I have to be both my mother and my father. I have to imagine myself. I will dare to show my fangs, run after prey, make a great pounce that could rip the neck of an eagle in flight. All my life seems like an injustice. Though I am a mighty warrior, I am only allowed to fight a stuffed dog. Though I possess strong jaws, I can only crush nutritious biscuits suggested by a vet who couldn't even smell a canary. This must end. I remain motionless—if necessary hanging by the tail like a lamp—in order to overcome my obstacles and my incapacity to act. The truth is that I no longer know what I want. It is impossible to choose what I like, not because I do not dare to, but because I don't know what I like. They have turned me into a domestic plaything. Food is placed before me, a flattened mash without smell or flavor. I do not know the taste of fresh blood spilling from a wound that my claws have made. Would I love it? Would it disgust me? A mystery. Before I move, I must enter the depths of my being and find out who I really am.

If you have drawn this card, it could mean:

Stillness, waiting, gestation, doubt, looking from another perspective, deep meditation, hiding something.

XIII
(Arcana without a name)

Everything that begins ends. I have had everything that one could wish for. The wealth of my masters was such that they put a gold and diamond collar around my neck. They reserved a sumptuous room just for me decorated with cushions of silk and velvet. I had a private chef who prepared delicious food for me and a servant who brushed my black coat to make it shine like the moon. It made me pretentious, full of disdain toward my friends, and I ended up feeling like a human. One day I suddenly understood I was a lonely feline. I was what my masters wished me to be, not what I actually was: an animal thirsty for space, for freedom, for blood on my teeth and my claws. Tearing off the collar that made me a slave, I swore to break the ties that bound me to my masters.

I manifested my rebellion by soaking the clothes in the wardrobe in urine, and I defecated in the bath. When they tried to punish me, I bit them. How quickly their great love turned to disdain! They took me far from the city and abandoned me in a rubbish dump. Halleluiah, my transformation had begun! Enormous rats attacked me. The anger accumulated in me from suppressing my wild nature for so long expressed itself in a devastating explosion. I transformed those rodents into rich nourishment.

The value system of my luxurious but artificial life was abolished. The sought-after perfumes of my old life became loathsome. Nothing compared to the odors of filth, no gourmet dish could compete with hot flesh chewed by powerful teeth. Now that I really am myself, I am happy. Full of the energy that was repressed for years, I am not ashamed to be the dump queen.

If you have drawn this card, it could mean:

Eliminate all that impedes your forward progress, leave aggression behind, mental cleansing, radical purification, rebirth, revolution, the end of an illusion.

TEMPERANCE

It is useless to ask me what my gender is: neither male nor female, I am a feline angel. I have come from heaven to be near you, to protect you, and to give you good advice. My body is covered in fine white fur and I have two great wings at my back. On my forehead blooms a flower of light, because my thoughts are pure and fragrant. My whiskers are antennae that capture the voice of Cat God.

My tail, long and silky, yet with muscles of steel, scares away not only flies but also evil temptations. I am your faithful guardian. You cannot imagine how many times I have saved you—from dangerous dogs, and cat trappers who want your fur, and trucks that continuously try to run you over. I love you infinitely. Have faith in me.

I am that inner voice that cries "Look out!" and helps you avoid the fatal mistake of trusting a feral cat that will steal the food you have hidden. Or that stops you from climbing a roof that is about to collapse, or caterwauling insults at a bulldog (an irreversible act that would put all of your nine lives in danger). I communicate with Nature so that she prevents an unexpected downpour when you go hunting in the countryside or huge winds that could blow you over the edge while you are walking on the terrace of a large building.

I am near you also to encourage you to act when the action is good, such as making you jump on a sparrow when it is distracted for a moment or pointing out the rubbish bin that has tasty fish bones. You are not alone. I am always watching over you. When you need something, pray to me by meowing loudly: "Intercede for me so that the Cat God will help me overcome this difficulty." All will be arranged.

If you have drawn this card, it could mean:
Protection, harmony, healing, a positive change, peace, mental balance.

THE DEVIL

I have claws and teeth like daggers and great wings like a bat. My body is covered with thick black hair like the mane of a horse. I have horns on my head and hooves for feet. The ugliest things do not scare me. Quite the opposite, they delight me. I can urinate sulfuric acid and defecate black turds that are meters long. I can live in tombs teeming with worms and devour huge tarantulas. I am a demon who has come to tempt you! I know that you who seems to be a docile and housebound animal in reality hides profound desires. Your ancestors were tigers who did not hesitate to feed upon monkeys, antelopes, snakes, humans. Poor little you, they have domesticated you to the point where you don't scratch furniture, you don't climb on the cupboards, you don't rip pages out of books or poke your nose in the children's food. You have be taught to be quiet when the grandmothers pray and you don't lick the statues of their saints.

If you give me your soul, I propose to hypnotize your masters and their servants. They won't be able to see you as you tear the curtains, destroy the cushions with your teeth, lap up the baby's milk, mix your gastric regurgitations with their food, and—the supreme pleasure—start a fire and burn everything down.

We will take their money. And you, transformed for a while into human form, will gamble in casinos and get drunk with women covered in glitter and makeup. You will murder the innocent and eat their viscera and become the being your master never permitted you to be. You will know yourself and understand you have immense possibilities. You will enrich the world with your creative fire. And when you return to your feline body, I will turn into the most beautiful of cats and I will show you what passion is. You will return to your original wild self. You will be happy to pay for all of this with your soul, your entire soul, which is so utterly domesticated that it is a useless ornament.

If you have drawn this card, it could mean:

Forbidden, dark forces of the subconscious, bestiality, artistic creativity, liberation of inhibitions, recognition of desires, accumulation of money.

THE TOWER

My twin brother and I were born in a castle in the shape of a tower, built in a beautiful valley full of trees and flowers, near a sparkling river. Our mother, an elegant Siamese cat, went to heaven having bought us into the world after a long labor. The two daughters of the master adopted us as if we were their own babies. They loved us so much that we were never allowed to leave the castle. We lived for several years closed inside, well fed, stroked and combed, and loved. Nevertheless, sadness weighed on us. We were forbidden to hunt, to bite, to scratch, and to meow. Hypocritically, we purred to make our owners believe we were happy in our luxurious prison.

Suddenly, a catastrophe came to our rescue. A storm of terrifying intensity erupted. The thunder was deafening, and the sky was filled with blinding bolts of lightning. One of these struck the roof of the castle and caused it to explode. My brother and I, who had been hiding there, fell headfirst into the void.

In the air, we turned so we could land on our paws. The storm ended and the shining sun appeared. Happy and safe, we were free and we looked at the world with new eyes. We were enchanted by the smell of the grass, by the heady perfumes of flowers, by the sugary flavor of the butterflies we swallowed, by the joy of climbing the trees and jumping from branch to branch, by the pride we felt scaring the birds and making the rabbits run away, and by the freshness of the water we enthusiastically drank from the river. Everything that was imprisoned in our souls emerged in the outside world. Now, receiving no orders, we live in life itself. Not in safety and boredom, but in uncertainty and elation, in the never-ending and wonderful struggle to survive. By the power of heaven and earth, the disaster made it clear that the world is our ally.

If you have drawn this card, it could mean:
Liberation, rupture, explosion of joy, necessary destruction, overcoming limits, enlightenment, being who you are.

THE STAR

The Cat God gave me a slender body and long legs, silken fur, elegant ears, and eyes the color of emeralds. Pretentious, selfish, haughty, I believed myself to be the center of the world. I was forever dissatisfied and instead of sharing I always demanded that more be given to me. I became so awful that I lost everything. I was thrown out of the house, which I had assumed was my exclusive property. I wandered, desperate, in inhospitable corners and fed myself on cockroaches, ants, and flies. After a long time, I came to a park where hunting was prohibited. Disgusting, all skin and bones, depressed, I raised my head and for the first time looked at the starry sky. The grandeur of this spectacle made me realize how small I was. I was ashamed to have wasted my energy by only loving myself.

I understood that I was united with the world, like a tiny gear in a great machine full of light. I became the messenger of that light. I received it and I shared it. I dug my claws into the earth and pulled out poisonous grass to make way for beautiful flowers. I removed the rubbish that polluted the waters of a stream. I conquered my carnivorous instincts and became a friend of birds, squirrels, and butterflies. Bees offered me their honey—food that allowed me to maintain my beauty and to survive without murdering.

I found my place on earth and my connection with the vast cosmos. My breasts were filled with milk, and this white river nourished many small orphan animals. My odorless excrement fertilized the earth and gave life to many fruit trees where the monkeys played and the nightingales sang.

I was transformed into a sacred cat, venerated by both plants and animals. Now I am happy. I give to the earth what the sky gives to me—a sublime energy that purifies the world.

If you have drawn this card, it could mean:
Finding purpose, purity, forgiveness, sacred submission, communion with the cosmos, fertility.

THE MOON

Each night, my beloved cat, curled up on the roof of your house, nose pointed toward the sky, you gaze at me with your big yellow eyes. You are fascinated by my splendor. You want to know my mystery, to know why I grow and diminish and grow again. You want to know why you feel strange when I am full, as if I were a magnet pulling another you from the secret depths of your soul, a feline that possesses unsettling desires and powers.

Know this: I represent the Cosmic Mother. Just as the universe has a father, it also has a mother. The father is called Sun, the mother, Moon. And it is she I represent. I am the ruler of dreams, of the imagination, of all that is hidden in you, that mysterious force that will make you a magician. When you have learned spiritual humility from me—the same humility that allows me to transform myself into an empty sphere with nothing that belongs to me, to be able to reflect the marvelous light of the Sun—you will know that your mind can do the same. It can purify itself from useless words and be filled with a power that comes from your soul. It is called intuition. If you are able to awaken it, you will become a poet, a wise reader of the tarot, a healer, a clairvoyant.

I shine in the darkness of night as a silver disc. I do not create, I merely indicate. Those who receive my light know what it means, nothing more. Beneath my light, a human is human, a ferocious beast is ferocious, madness is madness. And a beautiful cat such as yourself is beautiful. I am the mirror of all that exists.

Have you understood? Look at me and begin to see. You are not alone, you are not crazy, you are not a useless animal. Nor are you a little anguished mind. You are an important part of this world, you have natural wisdom and a spirit without limits. You are the light that your arrogant masters vaguely suspect reigns in the depths of their blind souls.

If you have drawn this card, it could mean:

Intuition, receptiveness, divination, imagination, madness, solitude, an ideal that should be sought.

THE SUN

You, big orange-furred cat, you stretch out on the desert wasteland, belly up, in a patch of earth heated by my light. When your starving brothers arrive, you hiss, growl, flex your claws and show your teeth to chase them away from this uniquely pleasant place. You think I belong exclusively to you. But you are wrong! I, the Sun, the source of heat and light, I am the father of all living beings and there is not one whose life does not depend on me. Don't think just because your coat is almost the same color as me that you mean more than the others. I distribute my rays without refusing anyone. I love everyone the same way.

I burn in the sky, always giving of myself, asking nothing in return. This is why I wish that you would vanquish your selfishness and learn to share, uniting with your fellows in a relationship of mutual help. You survive in this wasteland because you have more intelligence and more strength than the others. They are simple felines and think only of finding something to fill their stomachs and to sleep hidden away where no dog will attack them. But you wish to be the head of a large family, to liberate your children and travel until you find a bountiful forest where they can become powerful tigers again.

For this to happen, you need to learn to help those who are less aware than you. You must not only be the father to your own children but to all wandering cats. You must become a prophet, offer them a better future, give them hope. Instead of living in desolation, they can be their own masters in a fertile world where they can begin a new and happy life. Like me, you must cultivate unconditional love in your heart and an absolute desire of a collective dream.

But beware of excess power! If I don't hold back, I can provoke fires and drought, and transform the entire planet into a desert. Oh, great orange cat, do not become a tyrant at the service of death rather than life!

If you have drawn this card, it could mean:
A happy union, a new life, love, brotherhood/sisterhood, success, evolution, construction.

JUDGEMENT

I am the Cat God's favorite angel. His messenger. I have come to give you good tidings: the four of you—mother, father, son, and daughter, idealistic cats who move through life's troubles, yearning for a better world where you are no longer domestic slaves but collaborators with your human owners, on equal footing—you will attain what you deserve!

Even though your owners have material power and a certain intelligence and articulated language, they also destroy forests, pollute rivers with their industrial waste, fill the oceans with rubbish, and poison the air. Yes, they are immensely powerful, but you, my beloved cats, have many things they lack. You are at home in the dark, and you can see the countless roaming phantoms who try in vain to communicate with the living. You know when an ill person will die. Your warmth and your purring soothe the lonely soul. Above all, you are an irreplaceable bridge between the ordinary industrious world and the magical world. You are able to attract fairies, elves, gnomes, mermaids, and so many other marvelous beings that dwell on this earth, which humans have transformed into such an inhospitable place.

Together, cats and humans will revive dead values such as alchemy, divination, mythical heroism, the manifestation of miracles, time travel to converse with ancestors. This could be the future because all beings aspire to a better world where goodness, imagination, and beauty reign. In the meantime, the Cat God will give you wings and haloes. You will be transformed into angel cats, and with constant joy you will sow peace and knowledge. You will proclaim that life is worth living, and that felines and humans, together, will make the planet the most beautiful garden imaginable.

If you have drawn this card, it could mean:
Awareness, triumph, a happy family, rebirth, transformation, a future project, universal love.

THE WORLD

At the beginning of my long search for understanding, my crazy female cat friend pushed me to give up everything and wander like an illuminated beggar. She was convinced that the most important thing in life was to have freedom, to empty one's mind, to possess nothing, to sort of fade away.

But I found over the years that I possessed an immense treasure: myself. I freed myself from

self-destruction. I recognized the deep wisdom bequeathed to me by countless ancestors. I stopped living as a prisoner of my own egoism and I pitied the suffering of those like me, slaves to their own animalism. I placed myself at the service not only of the feline race but of all living beings on earth, including vegetal beings.

Today I am laying consciousness before you. Observe yourself. Realize that you live in a body that will change, grow old, and then disappear so your spirit can visit other wonderful worlds. As long as you have it, nourish it well. Lick yourself clean from your whiskers to your tail. Exercise, dance, fight, overcome difficulties with the strong intention of becoming a hero capable of doing miracles for those like you. You will command your emotions, cleansing your heart of lusts, of anger and jealousy and the desire to sink your teeth into defenseless others. You will fill your heart with love. You will help kittens and masters to better understand each other, and you will share your food with the lost ones who have none.

You will develop your mind to its maximum potential. You will learn to talk like humans and teach them many things they have forgotten as prisoners of the cities—to survive in a virgin forest, to talk with ancient wise phantoms. You will develop your sexual energy and use it not only to give life to a happy family with the cat you love but also to create sublime works of art. When humans and cats come to see you, full of admiration, you can say to them: "There is nothing in me that is not also in you. How can you say no to a universe that says yes? Dance with me! Savor the supreme happiness, which is the happiness of living! It's a grand party! The Cat God created the world so that we can love it as much as he loves us!"

If you have drawn this card, it could mean:
Success, fullness, supreme realization, perfection, spirit of the world, ecstasy, holiness.

APPENDIX

Tarot of Cats and Tarot of Marseille

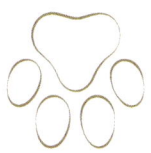

THE FOOL THE MAGICIAN

THE HIGH PRIESTESS THE EMPRESS

THE EMPEROR

THE HIEROPHANT

THE LOVER

THE CHARIOT

JUSTICE

THE HERMIT

THE WHEEL OF FORTUNE   STRENGTH

   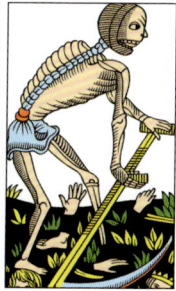

THE HANGED MAN   XIII

  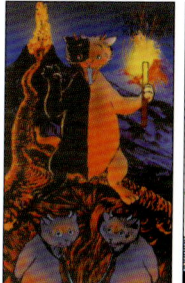 

TEMPERANCE   THE DEVIL

THE TOWER   THE STAR

THE MOON   THE SUN

JUDGEMENT   THE WORLD

BIOGRAPHY

Alejandro Jodorowsky

Alejandro Jodorowsky (Chile, 1929) is an eclectic artist, writer of plays, novels and comic books, and a movie and theatre director. In the world of Tarot, Jodorowsky is one of the greatest masters of the XX century. A lifelong scholar of the *Tarot de Marseille*, he has written some of the most important books on the subject, in particular *The Way of the Tarot*, and *I, the Tarot*, as well as *The way Jodorowsky explained Tarot to his Cat*.

In 1955, Jodorowsky went to Paris to study as a mime under the teaching of Marcel Marceau. Here he worked with Maurice Chevalier, with whom he made a short film entitled *La cravate* (1957), and frequented the surrealists Roland Topor and Fernando Arrabal, writing numerous books and plays, and founding with them, in 1962, the "Panic Movement" - in homage to the god Pan. At the end of the sixties he directed avant-garde theatres in Paris and Mexico City, and made his first movie: a surreal love story entitled *Fando and Lis* (1968), based on a text by Arrabal. In 1970 he directed the film *El topo* and 3 years later *The Holy Mountain*.

In 1975 he returned to France to work on a movie from the adaptation of Frank Herbert's *Dune*, with Orson Welles, David Carradine, Salvador Dalí among others, music by Pink Floyd, ideas by H.R. Giger, Dan O'Bannon and Moebius. The project failed and would then be realized by David Lynch. From the early eighties he begins to work with Moebius and other artists on graphic novels and comics, writing at the same time numerous books, almost all now of international fame. He returned to directing with *Santa Sangre* (1989) and in 1990 he directed Omar Sharif and Peter O'Toole in *The Rainbow Thief*.

The themes of Tarot, always dear to him, echo in *The Dance of Reality* and *Psychomagia: a Panic Therapy*, in which of theatre is directed towards a metaphorical magic through Tarot and rituals related to them.

Jodorowsky now lives in Paris, where he continues his study of the Tarot de Marseille, in particular of the Minor Arcana.

FOREWORD AUTHOR
Daniele Palmieri

Daniele Palmieri (born November 1994), a graduate in Philosophical Sciences and a student of esoteric studies, is as passionate about Tarot as he is about cats. To the first passion he dedicated his book *The Tarot and the Initiation Tradition* (Tlon Edition) and to the second his series composed of *Diary of a Cynical Cat*, *The Story of a Librarian Cat*, and *The Cat, the Magician and the Inquisitor* (Magazzini Salani Editore).